Transport Around the World

Trains

Chris Oxlade

Heinemann
LIBRARY

www.heinemann.co.uk
Visit our website to find out more information about Heinemann Library books.

To order:
 Phone 44 (0) 1865 888066
 Send a fax to 44 (0) 1865 314091
 Visit the Heinemann Bookshop at www.heinemann.co.uk to browse our catalogue
and order online.

First published in Great Britain by Heinemann Library,
Halley Court, Jordan Hill, Oxford OX2 8EJ, part of Pearson Education.
Heinemann is a registered trademark of Pearson Education Ltd.

Editorial: Diyan Leake and Kristen Truhlar
Design: Kimberley R. Miracle and Ray Hendren
Picture research: Erica Martin
Production: Julie Carter

Originated by Chroma Graphics (Overseas) Pte Ltd
Printed and bound in China by South China Printing Co. Ltd

ISBN 978 0 4310 8701 6 (hardback)
12 11 10 09 08
10 9 8 7 6 5 4 3 2 1

ISBN 978 0 4310 8711 5 (paperback)
12 11 10 09 08
10 9 8 7 6 5 4 3 2 1

British Library Cataloguing in Publication Data
Oxlade, Chris
Transport Around the World: Trains

A full catalogue record for this book is available from the British
Library.

Acknowledgements
The publishers would like to thank the following for permission to
reproduce photographs: Alamy pp. **6** (Martin Bond), **17** (Iain Masterton);
R.D. Battersby p. **16**; Steve Benbow p. **14**; Sylvia Cordaiy pp. **7**, **8**, **23**,
27; Digital Vision p. **24**; Eye Ubiquitous pp. **4**, **11**; Getty Images p. **10**
(Stone/Richard A. Cooke, III), **28** (National Geographic/Justin Guariglia);
James Davis Travel Photography p. **18**; Milepost p. **25**; PA Photos
p. **15**; Pictures p. **13**; QA Photos p. **20**; Quadrant pp. **12**, **21**, **26**;
Science Photo Library p. **29**; SNCF p. **19**; Tony Stone Images pp. **5**, **9**;
VSOE p. **22**.

Cover photograph of a bullet train reproduced with permission of
Getty Images/Taxi (Michael Dunning).

The publishers would like to thank Carrie Reiling for her assistance in
the publication of this book.

Every effort has been made to contact copyright holders of any material
reproduced in this book. Any omissions will be rectified in subsequent
printings if notice is given to the publishers.

Contents

Some words are shown in bold, **like this**. You can find out what
they mean by looking in the glossary.

What is a train?

A train is a machine that moves along on metal rails. Passengers travel inside the train's **carriages**. The carriages are pulled along by a **locomotive**.

A train can have many carriages or just a few.

carriages

A train driver sits in a small **cab** at the front of the locomotive. There are handles and pedals to make the train start and stop. They also make the train speed up and slow down.

There are many instruments in the cab to help the driver drive the train.

How trains work

wires

80

locomotive

The wires above the track give power to an electric train.

Some trains are **electric** trains. Electric motors in the **locomotive** make its wheels turn round to move the train along. The electricity comes from wires above the track.

This locomotive uses diesel fuel to power the engine.

Some trains have a **diesel** locomotive. It has a huge **engine** called a diesel engine. The engine needs **fuel** to make it work.

Old trains

barrel

Water was carried in the barrel at the back of this locomotive. The water was heated by the engine to make steam.

Early trains used **steam** for power. The first steam **locomotive** was called the Rocket. It was built in 1829 and carried passengers between Liverpool and Manchester in England.

This is a large steam locomotive.

Monster steam locomotives had very powerful **engines**. They pulled **freight** trains with hundreds of wagons of **cargo** across the United States in the 1940s.

Steam trains

In some countries trains are still pulled by **steam locomotives**. Inside the locomotive there is a roaring fire. This makes water boil to make steam.

Steam locomotives still carry passengers and **cargo** in some countries.

Trains need enormous engines and wheels to pull heavy cargo long distances.

On a steam locomotive, steam makes **pistons** move in and out. Long rods are attached to the pistons. The rods make the wheels spin round.

Where trains are used

Trains can only be used where there is a track laid for them. Most tracks are made up of two metal rails. Coloured lights called signals tell train drivers when to stop or go.

This train can switch from one track to another.

signals

Railway tracks go between towns and cities. They go from station to station. Passenger trains stop at stations to let passengers get on and off.

Passenger trains like this one only carry people and their luggage. They do not carry **cargo**.

Going to work by train

Every day millions of people travel to work and school on **commuter** trains. These trains stop at most stations. They pick up passengers and take them into city centres.

Commuter trains often run only during working hours.

Commuter trains have lots of wide doors so that the passengers can get on and off quickly. There are seats inside the **carriages**. There is also space for passengers to stand if all the seats are taken.

Railway stations are busy places.

Underground trains

This underground train is arriving at the station.

Underground trains travel through tunnels deep beneath the busy city streets. The stations where they stop are also under the ground. All underground trains are **electric** trains.

Underground trains avoid the busy traffic above ground. They can get very crowded during the rush hour. Inside the **carriages** there are plenty of handles for standing passengers to hold on to.

In some busy cities, **carriages** on underground trains get very crowded.

handles

Express trains

Express trains whizz along at more than 200 kilometres (125 miles) per hour. They carry people quickly between cities. The famous Japanese "bullet train" is an express train.

This bullet train is travelling past Mount Fuji in Japan.

Express trains like this one travel quickly between cities.

The front of an express train has a smooth, **streamlined** shape. The train slices easily through the air. This helps it speed along.

Shuttle trains

tunnel

This shuttle train travels underneath the English Channel between England and France.

Shuttle trains go back and forth between two stations. Some of them carry cars and coaches on some of their wagons. Other wagons carry trucks.

Shuttle trains are often used as **commuter** trains between two countries.

Passengers drive their cars on to the shuttle at one end of the journey. They can stay in their cars on the train. They drive off again when the train reaches the other end.

Luxury trains

Some long-distance trains are very **luxurious**. Passengers have their own **cabins** to sleep in overnight. The famous Orient Express is a luxury train.

The Orient Express travels through Europe and Asia.

A meal in a dining car on a luxury train is a special event.

On a luxury train the passengers eat their meals in a special **carriage** called a dining car. It is like a restaurant on wheels. Meals are cooked in part of the car called the galley.

Freight trains

A **freight** train carries **cargo** instead of passengers.
The cargo is carried in special wagons. Each wagon is
connected to the next one with a hook called a coupling.

When freight trains instead of lorries
carry cargo, it means that less space
on roads is taken up.

Railway tracks are built on a layer of small pieces of rock called ballast. Special freight wagons can spread new ballast when it is needed. A hole in the bottom of the wagon opens to let the ballast out.

ballast

ballast

This train spreads new ballast on the track where it is needed.

Mountain trains

Mountain trains can go up much steeper hills than other trains. The **engine** of a mountain train must work very hard to climb the mountains. Mountain railways also need special tracks.

This train is climbing up the Alps, a mountain range that goes through France, Italy, and Switzerland.

rack

A mountain train needs a rack
to pull it up the steep track.

Mountain railway tracks have a rack between the rails.
Locomotives have an extra wheel that fits into the rack.
It stops the train sliding back down the steep track.

Maglev trains

The word *maglev* is short for *magnetic levitation*. This means "being held in the air by magnets". A maglev train floats just above its track because of magnetic levitation.

Maglev trains can travel as fast as bullet trains.

A trip in a maglev train is very fast and comfortable.

There are very strong magnets in a maglev track and train. They push against each other. This forces the train upwards and forwards. Maglev trains are fast and quiet.

Timeline

1803   British engineer Richard Trevithick builds the first **steam locomotive**.

1830   The first passenger railway is opened in England between Liverpool and Manchester. The trains are pulled by a steam locomotive called the Rocket.

1863   The world's first underground railway is opened in London.

1879   The first **electric** locomotive is demonstrated in Berlin, Germany.

1883   The luxury train the Orient Express makes its first journey between Paris, France and Istanbul, Turkey.

1940s   Enormous Big Boy locomotives are built in the United States for pulling **cargo** trucks. Each one weighed 600 tonnes.

1981   In France the TGV express train makes its first journey between the cities of Paris and Lyon.

1982   A maglev railway is opened at Birmingham airport, England.

2004   Two Spanish companies make train wheels that can change widths. This helps trains run on different types of tracks in different countries.

Glossary

cab   space at the front of a locomotive where the train driver sits

cabin   private room on a train with beds for passengers

cargo   goods that are moved from place to place

carriage   long vehicle that rolls along a railway track with seats for passengers

commuter   person who travels to work by car or train

diesel   a type of heavy oil that some engines use

electric   using electricity to run

engine   machine that uses fuel to power movement

freight   cargo transported by train or ship

fuel   substance that burns to make heat

locomotive   vehicle with an engine or motor that pulls carriages or wagons along a railway track

luxurious   very comfortable

piston   rod that moves in and out of a cylinder

steam   water that has become a gas

streamlined   curved and smooth

Find Out More

All About Trains, Michael Harris (Southwater, 2004).

First Discovery: Trains, James Prunier (Moonlight, 2005).

Go Facts ... Transport: Trains, Ian Rohr (A & C Black, 2005).

I Dream of Trains, Angela Johnson (Simon & Schuster, 2003).

Travel Through Time: Riding the Rails, Jane Shuter (Raintree, 2005).

Index